Earth's Precious Resources

Fuels
ld depends on

Heinemann
LIBRARY

Ian Graham

www.heinemann.co.uk/library

Visit our website to find out more information about **Heinemann Library** books.

To order:

☎ Phone 44 (0) 1865 888066

▤ Send a fax to 44 (0) 1865 314091

▭ Visit the Heinemann Bookshop at www.heinemann.co.uk/library to browse our catalogue and order online.

First published in Great Britain by Heinemann Library, Halley Court, Jordan Hill, Oxford OX2 8EJ, part of Harcourt Education.
Heinemann is a registered trademark of Harcourt Education Ltd.

© Harcourt Education Ltd 2004
First published in paperback in 2005
The moral right of the proprietor has been asserted.

Editorial: Andrew Farrow and Dan Nunn
Design: David Poole and Paul Myerscough
Picture Research: Melissa Allison and Andrea Sadler
Production: Duncan Gilbert

Originated by Ambassador Litho Ltd
Printed in China by WKT Company Limited

ISBN 0 431 11550 8 (hardback)
08 07 06 05 04
10 9 8 7 6 5 4 3 2 1

ISBN 0 431 11558 3 (paperback)
09 08 07 06 05
10 9 8 7 6 5 4 3 2 1

British Library Cataloguing in Publication Data

Graham, Ian
  Fossil fuels: a resource our world depends on. – (Earth's precious resources)
  1. Fossil fuels – Juvenile literature
  I. Title
  553.2
A full catalogue record for this book is available from the British Library.

Acknowledgements

The publishers would like to thank the following for permission to reproduce photographs: BryantMole Books p. **15 bottom right**; Corbis pp. **10** (Hulton-Deutsch Collection), **12** (Craig Aurness), **15 bottom left**; Corbis SABA p. **28** (David Buton); Corbis Sygma p. **23** (Jacques Langevin); Ecoscene pp. **19** (Pat Groves), **27** (Jim Winkley); Getty Images pp. **15 top** (Photodisc), **20 bottom** (Photodisc), **26** (Photodisc); Harcourt Education Ltd p. **4 top** (Simon Girling Associates/James Field); NASA p. **11 top**; PA Photos pp. **6, 7, 16, 20 top, 29**; Robert Harding Picture Library p. **17 bottom**; Science Photo Library pp. **4 bottom** (CSIRO/Geoff Lane), **18** (Martin Bond); Topham Picturepoint pp. **9, 14** (ImageWorks), **17 top** (ImageWorks), **22** (ImageWorks), **24** (AP), **25** (ImageWorks).

Cover photograph reproduced with permission of Getty Images/Photodisc.

Every effort has been made to contact copyright holders of any material reproduced in this book. Any omissions will be rectified in subsequent printings if notice is given to the publishers.

The paper used to print this book comes from sustainable resources.

Contents

Any words appearing in the text in bold, **like this**, are explained in the Glossary.

What are fossil fuels?

Fossil fuels are natural resources found in the ground. They are coal, oil and natural gas. They formed from plants and animals that died hundreds of millions of years ago. We release the energy they contain by burning them.

What is coal?

Coal is all that remains of forests that once grew on most of the Earth. When the trees died and fell, they were buried under soil and mud. First, they turned into peat, a spongy material that can be dried and burned. As more earth built up on top of the peat, all the water and air were squeezed out and it slowly hardened and turned into coal.

Some of the forests that formed the coal we use today were growing even before the dinosaurs walked the Earth.

Millions of years of being squashed underground changed dead plants into coal.

What is oil?

Oil is a sticky black liquid formed from the remains of tiny plants and animals, called plankton. They lived in the sea millions of years ago. When they died, they sank to the seabed, where they were covered by mud before they could rot. Over millions of years, heat and the action of **microbes** changed them into oil.

What is natural gas?

Natural gas is a mixture of gases found underground. It is mostly made from a gas called methane. Three other gases – ethane, propane and butane – are mixed with it. Natural gas usually forms in the same places as oil. It may be dissolved in the oil, like the bubbles in a fizzy drink. Or it may rise to the top of the oil and become trapped under the rock above it.

Oil and gas become trapped between layers of rock.

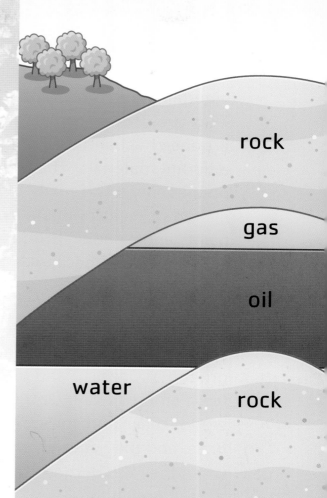

rock

gas

oil

water

rock

Why are fossil fuels important?

The way we live today depends on using huge amounts of energy for heating, lighting, **industry**, transport and entertainment. Most of this is supplied by fossil fuels. They are used in two main ways. They are burned to produce heat and they are **processed** to make lots of different materials. The plastic parts of toys, mobile phones, pens and many of the other things we use in our everyday lives are made from fossil fuels. Many of the paints and cleaning products we use in our homes are made from fossil fuels too.

Fossil fuels are also important because of their effect on the environment. They are **extracted** from the ground, processed and used in huge amounts all over the world. Leaks and spills of fossil fuels, and the gases produced when they are burned, cause a lot of pollution.

Fossil fuels have many uses. In a supermarket, plastic packaging and signs, the flooring and even some of the clothes worn by the staff are made from fossil fuels, mainly oil. The electricity that powers the fridges, freezers, lighting and heating comes from fossil fuels too.

What is the heat from fossil fuels used for?

The heat given off by burning fossil fuels is used in different ways. It is used to keep buildings warm. It is used in power stations to make electricity. It is also used to make engines and other machines work.

Did you know?

Natural gas was discovered by ancient peoples. The ancient Chinese used natural gas as fuel to boil salty water. They wanted salt, which was left behind after the water had boiled away. The ancient Greeks and Romans used natural gas seeping from the ground to make eternal (never-ending) flames for their **temples** and **shrines**.

Air travel depends on the fossil fuels burned in aircraft engines.

Where are fossil fuels found?

Fossil fuels are not found everywhere. Coal is found where vast forests grew millions of years ago. Oil and natural gas are found where the ground was once at the bottom of **prehistoric** oceans.

Where are coal and gas found?

Coal is the most widespread fossil fuel. It is found in more places than oil or natural gas. Some countries which produce a lot of coal include Russia, Ukraine, the USA and China.

The biggest natural **gas fields** are found in Russia and the Middle East. One of the biggest, the Urengoy field, was found in Russia in the 1960s. The gas is trapped under rock more than 1000 metres (3280 feet) below the ground.

Coal is found in every **continent**.

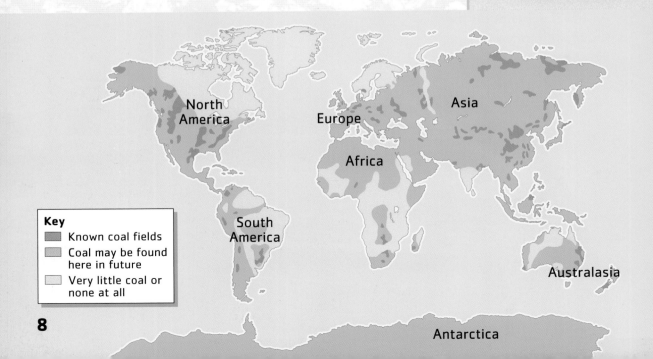

North America

Europe

Asia

Africa

South America

Australasia

Antarctica

Key
- Known coal fields
- Coal may be found here in future
- Very little coal or none at all

Where are the biggest oil fields?

The biggest **oil fields** are called supergiants. Only about 40 of the 50,000 oil fields found so far are supergiants. Most of them are in the Middle East, in countries such as Saudi Arabia and Iraq. Saudi Arabia produces more oil than any other country. It contains the world's biggest oil field, called Al-Ghawar. Al-Ghawar is 250 kilometres (155 miles) long and 35 kilometres (22 miles) wide.

The fuel business

The international trade in fossil fuels is one of the world's biggest businesses. Fossil fuels are sold by countries that have a lot of them, such as the USA and Russia, to other countries that have little or no fossil fuels of their own, such as France, Belgium, Armenia and Iceland. Countries with the most fossil fuels, especially oil-rich countries in the Middle East, such as Saudi Arabia and Kuwait, have become very wealthy by selling them.

This is Ras Tanura oil terminal in Saudi Arabia.

How are fossil fuels found?

Some fossil fuels are found lying on top of the ground. The sea sometimes wears down the ground above coal. Pieces of coal break off and the tide washes them onto the seashore. This is called sea coal.

In some places, a thick oily material called **asphalt** forms pools where oil oozes up out of the ground. These pools are also called tar pits and pitch lakes. Some of these pits and lakes have existed for millions of years. One in Los Angeles, USA, contains the remains of **prehistoric** animals that became stuck in the thick oil and died. Pitch Lake in Trinidad, in the West Indies, is so big that it contains millions of tonnes of asphalt. Asphalt collected from Pitch Lake is used in road-building.

Most fossil fuels are buried under the ground, so they have to be found in other ways.

Did you know?

Coal was burned in London for the first time in the year 1228. It was sea coal collected on the seashore in Scotland and northern England. People still collect coal from the seashore today.

How are buried fossil fuels found?

Scientists called geologists find buried fossil fuels by studying rocks on the ground, looking for the types of rocks that are often found in the same places as fossil fuels. They use photographs of the ground taken from aeroplanes and **satellites** to find the right rocks.

A satellite in space takes photographs that show a huge area of the ground.

Geologists learn more about rock hidden underground by banging the ground or setting off explosions. The sounds travel down into the ground and bounce back up from different layers of rock. The longer a sound takes to bounce back, the deeper the rock must be. This is called a **seismic** survey. Finally, people drill into the ground to see if fossil fuels are really there.

Sounds sent down into the ground bounce off the different layers of rocks and give scientists clues about what lies deep underground.

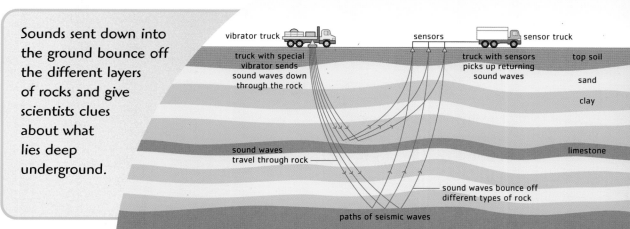

vibrator truck

sensors

sensor truck

truck with special vibrator sends sound waves down through the rock

truck with sensors picks up returning sound waves

top soil

sand

clay

sound waves travel through rock

limestone

sound waves bounce off different types of rock

paths of seismic waves

How are fossil fuels extracted?

Coal is dug out of the ground. Some coal is so near the surface that it can be reached by scraping away the ground on top of it. This makes a huge hole in the ground, which is called an open-cast **mine**.

Underground

Usually, coal is much deeper underground. Miners dig down to the coal and use machines to cut it away from the rock. As the miners tunnel through the coal, they prop up the roof to stop the rock above from falling down on top of them.

Coal mining is very dirty and dangerous work. In some mines, big machines can be used to cut out the coal. In others, miners like this man have to drill it out themselves.

Drilling for oil and gas

Oil and gas are reached by drilling down through the ground. Some oil and gas lie underneath the seabed. Drilling platforms, called rigs, stand in the sea. A rig has a tall tower, called a derrick, to hold a drill pipe. An engine spins the pipe so that a sharp drill at the end of it cuts through the ground.

As the drill cuts deeper, more lengths of pipe are added at the top to push it down even further. When it reaches oil or gas, they flow up through the drill hole to the surface. Drilling derricks are used in the same way on land.

Did you know?

One of the world's tallest oil rigs stands in the Gulf of Mexico. It is 1000 metres tall. That is more than three times the height of the Eiffel Tower in Paris. Its drill goes 5000 metres down below the seabed. That's greater than the height of Mont Blanc, the highest mountain in Europe!

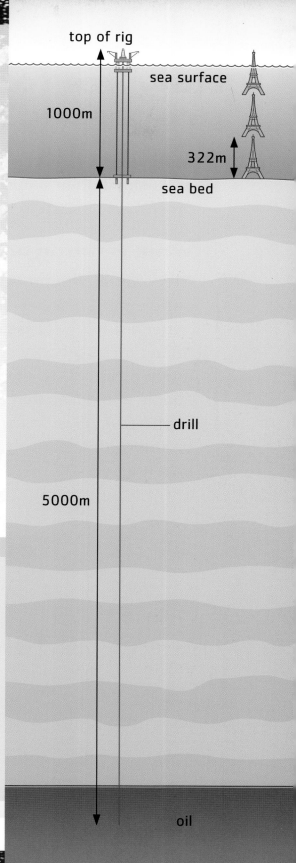

top of rig

sea surface

1000m

322m

sea bed

drill

5000m

oil

How are fossil fuels processed?

Fossil fuels are not taken straight out of the ground and used in their natural state. They have to be **processed** to change them into more useful materials.

What is crude oil?

Oil from the ground is also called crude oil, or petroleum. Crude oil is a mixture of lots of different materials. It is processed in a place called an oil refinery. The refinery's job is to change crude oil into a variety of different liquids and gases that are more useful. The oil is heated and treated with chemicals to split it up.

Oil refineries are huge factories. Oil companies try to use every part of the crude oil, so that none is wasted.

What is crude oil made into?

Many things are made from oil. The diesel oil, petrol and kerosene burned in car, ship and aircraft engines all come from oil. So do the chemicals that are used to make plastics, paints, washing-up liquids and synthetic (human-made) rubber. Some medicines, clothes and fertilizers (to help plants grow) are made from chemicals that come from oil. When all of these materials are taken out of crude oil, a sticky black material called bitumen is left. Even this is useful. Bitumen is used to make roads.

Did you know?

Clarinets and oboes are made from a material called ebonite. This is a very hard type of synthetic rubber. Car tyres are made from synthetic rubber too. And both are made from oil!

Rubber boots and car tyres are not made from natural rubber, which comes from trees. They are made from chemicals that come from oil. Many other objects around us are made from oil, too.

15

How are fossil fuels moved around?

Coal, oil and natural gas have to be moved from where they are found to where they are **processed**, and from there to where they are used. They are transported in a number of different ways.

How is coal transported?

Coal is carried away from the **coal face** by **conveyor belt** and then lifted to the surface. From there, it is transported by freight train, ship and truck. At power stations, coal is sometimes brought inside by a pipeline. To make it flow through the pipe, it is first mixed with water. Inside the power station, the water drains away and the coal is burned.

How are oil and gas moved?

Oil is transported by pipelines and **tankers**. The biggest oil tanker ships are called supertankers. Some of them are more than 400 metres (1300 feet) long.

The biggest oil tankers can each carry more than 100,000 tonnes of oil.

That's the same as four football pitches lying end to end.

Natural gas is transported by pipelines, special gas carrier ships and road tankers. Nearly all of the natural gas used today is moved by pipeline, flowing through the pipes as a gas. To transport natural gas by sea, it is cooled down to below −161.5 °C (−258.7 °F) so that it changes to a liquid, called liquid natural gas or LNG. When the ships arrive at their destination, the liquid is changed back to a gas by carefully warming it up.

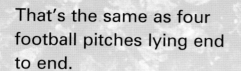

Transporting gas by pipeline, like this one in Alaska, is much easier than using hundreds of tanker trains and road tankers.

Once fossil fuels have been moved, they need to be stored. Coal can be piled up on the ground. Oil and gas are stored in tanks, like the gas tanks shown here.

How do power stations use fossil fuels?

Power stations are giant machines designed to produce electricity. They need energy to do it. Most power stations get the energy they need from coal, oil or natural gas.

A power station looks very complicated, but it carries out a series of very simple steps.

1 Coal, oil or natural gas is burned to produce heat.

2 The heat boils water in a tank, called a **boiler**, to make steam.

3 The steam blows through a machine called a **turbine** and makes it spin.

4 The spinning turbine drives a machine called a generator that actually makes the electricity.

Coal-fired power stations need a constant supply of coal, delivered by the train-load every day.

Did you know?

Energy cannot be made or destroyed. It can only be changed from one form into another. A power station changes the energy from its fuel into another form of energy – electricity.

CASE STUDY:
Drax power station, UK

The Drax power station near Selby, in northern England, is one of the world's biggest coal-fired power stations. Everything about the Drax power station is huge. Each of its six **boilers** is as tall as a fifteen-storey building. They burn up to 38,000 tonnes of coal every day. The coal is crushed to a fine powder so that it burns quickly.

How much electricity does Drax produce?

Drax supplies one-tenth of Britain's electricity needs. The amount of electricity produced by a big power station like Drax is measured in gigawatt-hours. One gigawatt-hour is an enormous amount of energy. It is enough to keep 700,000 light bulbs lit for a whole day and night. Drax produces about 24,000 gigawatt-hours of electricity every year.

Steam rises from the cooling towers of Drax power station.

How can extracting fossil fuels be dangerous?

Extracting fossil fuels from the ground is dangerous. **Mines** can collapse or flood with water. They can fill up with natural gas. There may be harmful dust in the air. Coal, oil and natural gas catch fire easily, so fire is a danger too.

Why is dust in coal mines harmful?

Dust in a coal mine is not the same as dust in your home. It contains tiny, sharp pieces of rock. If they are breathed in year after year, they can damage people's lungs and make it more difficult to breathe. Spraying water and blowing air through a mine helps to keep dust down.

Mining for coal is a very dirty and dangerous job.

Did you know?

Coal miners used to take birds underground with them. Poisonous gas in the mine would quickly affect the birds and warn the miners, giving them more time to escape.

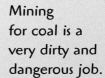

Why are there harmful gases in a coal mine?

As dead plants change into coal, gases are produced. When miners cut into the coal, any gas still there may escape into the mine. Most of it is a gas called methane. If this mixes with air, a spark can make it explode.

A poisonous gas called carbon monoxide is sometimes produced too. It can suffocate people. If another poisonous gas, called **hydrogen** sulphide, leaks into a mine, everyone knows about it right away, because it smells like rotten eggs!

The dangers of drilling

Drilling for gas is very dangerous. The gas must not be allowed to escape, because it catches fire very easily. Several gas platforms, which drill for gas under the sea, have been destroyed when leaking gas caught fire.

The Piper Alpha offshore oil rig, in the North Sea, was destroyed by a gas explosion and fire on 6 July 1988, killing 167 people.

How can using fossil fuels harm the environment?

Extracting and using fossil fuels causes pollution. Open-cast mining produces big, ugly holes in the land. **Mines**, oil wells and gas wells can produce lots of heavy traffic in places of great natural beauty.

Burning fossil fuels produces air pollution, which makes buildings dirty and affects people's health. Breathing in the smoke and fumes produced when fossil fuels are burned can make breathing disorders, such as asthma and bronchitis, worse. The smoke produced by burning fossil fuels, especially coal and oil, contains substances that can cause serious illnesses, such as cancer, if they are breathed in for a long time.

Heavy traffic produces so much smoke and fumes that the air in modern cities is often badly polluted.

How can fossil fuels harm the sea?

Accidents involving oil **tankers** and drilling rigs pollute the sea. Oil leaking from an oil tanker or an offshore oil well floats on top of the water. Seabirds that land in the oil become coated with it. They preen (clean) their feathers with their beaks and swallow so much oil that they often die. In time, the action of sunlight and the weather changes the oil and it sinks. When it reaches the seabed, it can kill the plants and sea creatures that live there. Close to the shore, it can kill or pollute shellfish, such as mussels, that are caught to be eaten. Oil washed up on the seashore covers it with a black, sticky, smelly layer.

The air over large parts of Kuwait was turned into a choking black fog in 1991 by burning oil wells during the first Gulf War.

Did you know?

Burning fossil fuels produces gases called greenhouse gases, which soak up heat from the Sun and warm the Earth. This could change the world's climate and weather, and produce more storms, floods and droughts.

CASE STUDY:
The Exxon Valdez oil spill

On 24 March 1989, the *Exxon Valdez* oil **tanker** strayed into shallow water in Prince William Sound, Alaska, USA. Rocks just under the surface ripped through the ship. About 39,000 tonnes of oil poured out. That's enough to fill 125 swimming pools. Wind and waves carried it onto the shore.

How did the oil affect wildlife?

Immediately after the spill, about 100 aircraft, 1000 boats and 10,000 people went to the region to try and save the wildlife. People sprayed the oil with chemicals to break it down and shovelled it up. Even so, about 250,000 birds, 2800 sea otters, 300 seals, and 22 whales are thought to have died. Billions of fish eggs probably died too. Wildlife takes a long time to recover from a disaster of this size. The numbers of some seabirds, seals, sea otters and shellfish had still not recovered more than ten years after the disaster.

The *Exxon Valdez* oil spill in Alaska killed hundreds of thousands of creatures.

Will fossil fuels ever run out?

Every year the world uses fossil fuels that took more than one million years to form. New fossil fuels are being made, but not quickly enough to keep up with our demand for them. One day they will run out.

How long will fossil fuels last?

Many scientists agree that all the **oil fields** we know about today will have run dry in about 40 years. **Gas fields** will last about 65 years. Oil and gas will actually last longer than this because new fields are still being found. Even so, a time will come when no new oil and gas fields will be found and the old fields will run out.

Coal will last far longer than oil or gas. The **coal fields** we know about today will last at least another 200 years.

We are using up the world's oil in our cars, trucks and power stations so fast that it will run out in the near future.

How can we conserve fossil fuels?

Although fossil fuels will eventually run out, we could make them last longer by using them more slowly. Turning off the lights when you leave a room and turning the heating in your home down a fraction would save a tiny amount of energy every day. If millions of people did the same thing, all the small savings would add up to a big saving in fossil fuels. Walking or riding a bike sometimes, instead of going everywhere by car, would save more fossil fuels. **Recycling** plastic things would help to reduce the amount of new plastic that has to be made from oil.

The family in this house has left out plastic and other waste ready to be collected for recycling.

We could burn less petrol and oil in vehicles. We could build houses that hold more heat inside, so less fuel has to be burned to keep them warm. We could make electricity in different ways, without burning coal, oil or gas. There are lots of options open to us.

How is electricity made without fossil fuels?

The wind, waves, tides, rivers, sunlight and even heat from deep underground can supply energy to make electricity. Unlike fossil fuels, these sources of energy will not run out. That is why this type of energy is called renewable energy.

Some electricity is already being made from renewable sources, mainly wind and water, but developing other sources of energy is very expensive. They must also produce electricity that is no more expensive for people to buy than electricity from fossil fuel power stations.

How can we use less petrol and oil?

We could make fewer journeys by car, by using buses and trains. Of course, buses and trains burn fuel too, but one full bus can replace dozens of car journeys, and one train can replace hundreds of car journeys. We could also drive cars with smaller engines, which burn less fuel, or with engines that use a different fuel.

Wind **turbines** like these in Denmark make electricity from the wind.

What kind of cars do not burn petrol or oil?

Electric cars are powered by electric motors instead of engines. Although they do not burn petrol or oil, the electricity that charges their **batteries** comes from power stations. Very little fossil fuel is saved. It is burned in power stations instead of cars.

A new type of electric car, powered by a **fuel cell** instead of a battery, is being designed (see the case study on page 29). A fuel cell makes electricity by combining **hydrogen** and oxygen.

There are also cars that use an electric motor for short, slow journeys and switch to a petrol engine for longer, faster journeys. These are known as hybrid cars.

Electric cars run on battery power instead of burning petrol or oil.

CASE STUDY:
The Mercedes-Benz fuel-cell car

The Mercedes-Benz A-Class 'F-Cell' car is a **prototype** car powered by a **fuel cell**. It can reach a speed of 100 kilometres (62 miles) an hour in 16 seconds and has a top speed of about 140 kilometres (85 miles) an hour. It can be driven a distance of about 300 kilometres (185 miles) on a full tank of **hydrogen**.

Why are there so few fuel-cell cars?

Fuel-cell cars are so new that they are still being tested. They are not yet ready to be sold to the public. Before they can go on sale, fuel stations will have to be fitted with new pumps so that fuel-cell cars can be re-fuelled as easily as any car today.

The Mercedes F-Cell looks like a normal car, but it is powered by a fuel cell instead of petrol.

Glossary

asphalt thick, black or dark brown liquid made from oil. Asphalt is also called tar and pitch. Natural asphalt is found in small pools or larger lakes where oil has oozed out of the ground.

battery small package of chemicals designed to produce a steady electric current

boiler tank where water is boiled to produce hot water or steam

coal face part of a coal mine where miners cut the coal away from the surrounding rock

coal field place under the ground where there is a lot of coal

continent one of the world's largest land areas. There are seven continents: Europe, North America, South America, Africa, Asia, Australasia and Antarctica.

conveyor belt endless loop of material driven by rollers and used to carry materials short distances

extract take something out of something else, often using industrial methods

fuel cell device that makes electricity from the chemical reaction between hydrogen and oxygen gases

gas field place under the ground that is rich in natural gas

hydrogen gas found in water and living things

industry businesses that extract and process materials and make goods

microbes tiny living creatures, so small that they can be seen only by using a microscope

mine/mining digging into the ground to reach valuable materials such as coal

oil field place under the ground that has lots of oil

prehistoric time before people started writing

process to change a material through a series of actions or treatments

prototype original model, the first example of a car, plane or any other product. Prototypes are built to test things, to make sure that they work properly.

recycling collecting materials that have been used at least once already and using them again

satellite small object that orbits around a larger object, such as a spacecraft going around the Earth

seismic shaking the ground, either by an earthquake or by human-made means, such as an explosion

shrine religious place where people pray

tanker a vehicle designed to carry a large amount of liquid

temple building where people worship their god or gods

turbine a type of wheel designed to spin very fast when it is driven by water, steam or gas

Find out more

Books

Fossil Fuels, Ian Graham (Wayland Publishers, 1998)

Fossil Fuels, Diane Gibson (The Creative Company, 2002)

Our Planet in Peril: Oil Spills, Jillian Powell (Franklin Watts, 2002)

Resources and the Environment: Oil, Ian Mercer (Franklin Watts, 2003)

World's Worst Oil Spills, Rob Alcraft (Heinemann Library, 2000)

Websites

www.schoolscience.co.uk/petroleum/index.html

Information about oil and the things that are made from it, from the Institute of Petroleum.

oils.gpa.unep.org/kids/kids.htm

Links to information about oil in the sea, natural gas, coal and other sources of energy, from the Global Marine Oil Pollution Information Gateway.

www.edisonthebus.org/energy.html

A guide to energy conservation.

www.consrv.ca.gov/dog/kids_teachers

Information about oil and natural gas in California, USA, from the California Department of Conservation.

Disclaimer

All the Internet addresses (URLs) given in this book were valid at the time of going to press. However, due to the dynamic nature of the Internet, some addresses may have changed, or sites may have ceased to exist since publication. While the author and publishers regret any inconvenience this may cause readers, no responsibility for any such changes can be accepted by either the author or the publishers.

Index